On My Brother's Shoulders

On My Brother's Shoulders

An African American Anthology and Tribute to People of Color

Poetry Written By: E. Willa Simpson
Story Edited By: E. Willa Simpson

An amazingly poetic tribute to countless African American legends; featuring
an intimate running dialogue with Angela Davis, Michael Eric Dyson, and
Howard Bingham: producer of major Motion Picture film "Ali," as they
share their unique experiences with critical moments in history; including
the brutal lynching of Emmett Till, a fourteen year old African American
youth that would serve as precursor to the early civil rights movement.

authorHOUSE®

AuthorHouse™ LLC
1663 Liberty Drive
Bloomington, IN 47403
www.authorhouse.com
Phone: 1-800-839-8640

The views expressed in this work are solely those of the author and do not necessarily reflect the views of the publisher, and the publisher hereby disclaims any responsibility for them.

This book is based on the academic (theoretical) examination of lynching. It is intended to help explain this social phenomena and to open up critical dialogue on the issue and the many meanings held by the term itself; by dissecting the ideology behind lynching along with the physical and psychological scars held by many African Americans as a direct result of generations of enslavement in the United States and the deaths of several key martyrs.

Published by AuthorHouse   12/20/2013

ISBN: 978-1-4184-2886-0 (sc)
ISBN: 978-1-4184-2887-7 (e)

This book is printed on acid-free paper.

TABLE OF CONTENTS

DEDICATED TO

My beloved little brother Rex, whom I will truly miss.

My loving parents who took the time to instill a great and solemn confidence within.

Sister Betty Shabazz and Minister Malcolm X for their unselfish contributions to the struggle.

Dr. Martin Luther King Jr. and Corretta Scott King for their unwavering commitment to non-violent change.

Dr. Maya Angelou for having the courage to sing.

Sojourner Truth for the strength that she passed down throughout generations and generations of Black women.

Harriet Tubman whose will we can never forget.

Oprah Winfrey for overcoming all of the odds and setting the standard for a "new" Black woman.

The great Billie Holiday who sang long before I ever knew the blues.

Paul Robeson for demonstrating that we can be successful at whatsoever we choose to do with our lives, so long as it's a good thing.

Bill and Camille Cosby for having the strong convictions and courage of heart to stand up to a nation.

Ruby Dee and Ossie Davis for exemplifying the lingering strength of the African bonds in marriage.

Angela Davis for being exactly and precisely who you are.

Congresswoman Maxine Waters for being willing to stand up for justice in every high and low place.

Myrlie Evers Williams who refused to give up.

Mamie Till Mobley for having the courage to take on the problems of this world.

Afeni Shakur for having the strength of heart to see your son's dream into a reality.

Professor Collins and Saul Lankster for acting as an inspirational catalyst for change.

Amiri whose love and support transformed my spirit and helped to shape me into the woman that I am today. I am a better person for just having known you and experienced your love.

Jenny for being an inspiration and a miracle to others all at the same time. You too have a great story to tell!

Malcolm Ali for being a friend, lifelong companion and representing the positive image of an African American father.

Harun for making a way out of no way for me. Thanks for all of your support!

John, Michelle, Carol and Rex whose love and support will get me through the most difficult of years.

My beloved little daughter who greatly changed my life when she entered into this world. You have truly blessed my life in so many ways that I could never have possibly imagined. If I don't live to see another day, my life has been worth it just because of you.

And last of all . . . to God and to all of those beautiful Black souls who have not refused to give up that resounding, awesome voice and continue to sing. *As on my brother's shoulders, I do emphatically, cry.*

INTRODUCTION

"On My Brother's Shoulders" is a collection of poetry and anthology written in memory of my youngest brother's passing away. It is a dedication to countless African American leaders that have contributed to the longevity of the African American race. It reflects the essence of the struggles that African Americans have faced in this country and the unique ability of African Americans to re-invent themselves in the face of conflict, oppression and strife.

There are so many unanswered questions pertaining to the unique experiences of African Americans living in this country and our uncharted plight. However, despite the many obstacles that have been presented to each generation of the African American race, we have still continued to succeed.

Many thanks to Angela Davis, Michael Eric Dyson, Howard Bingham, and Ernest Whithers whom each saw something of worth in this project and contributed unselfishly to its completion. My heart goes out to each of you and my prayer is that the truth of our history . . . Black History, American History will one day be heard and accepted for what it truly is, and taught accurately in the schools throughout this nation, and without risk of threats, brutality and senseless retaliation.

Many thanks also to Mamie Till Mobley for taking the time to speak with me about your son, Emmett Till. I enjoyed that moment more than any other time of my life (with the exception of giving birth to my daughter), and I am so very thankful for having had the opportunity to meet with you. I wish you peace on the journey now that you have transcended to a new and better life in heaven. I will always remember both you and your son, and your work will live on in spite of earthly limitations or barriers.

We are truly a people that have learned to live, breathe and sleep with struggle in the innermost cornerstone of our hearts. And yet, how truly thankful I am to God that we have held on to our faith and still continue to persevere in spite of all of the odds.

This blues filled, soul revealing work of art also serves as a chronology of the hopes, thoughts, fears and perseverance of the African American race. I have given this work to not only speak peacefully in laying my brother down to rest for a lifetime, however it was also constructed out of the mercy and goodwill that it would speak commandingly in the name of those who committed their lives to the struggle and to those beautiful proud Black souls who willingly laid down their lives for us.

This poetic collection of the Negro spiritual will hopefully become an inspiration to other African American souls, to pursue their own goals; whatsoever God has placed them here to do, until our paths meet again as one. I wish you all the best!

God Bless!
E. Willa Simpson

EVOLUTION OF LYNCHING

"The civil rights era was a very trying time in the history of the United States. It was a time when White Americans were violently divided on their feelings towards African Americans; and tensions were remarkably worse in the South. There were several laws, social mores and other discriminatory traditions established that were intentionally designed to keep the two races apart, but none had as significant an impact as the Brown vs. Board of Education decision of 1954 which outlawed the segregation of public schools and other public facilities. It was a critical decision that would soon make the separate but equal doctrine a distant memory from the past.

For one of the first times in the history of the United States, Supreme Court justices were finally beginning to publicly recognize the humanity of Blacks. Their ruling opened up countless opportunities to African Americans that could never have been possible in previous years. However, no matter how triumphant a victory this legal decision would prove itself to be for African Americans in general, many angry White Southerners felt as though they had somehow been betrayed by the American judicial system. While African Americans on the other hand felt like they had a friend who was looking out for them and as though maybe justice wasn't so terribly blind after all. Somehow, the future looked much brighter for them and their children. The former slaves and their descendants knew that there were going to be some major changes to take place as a direct result of the Supreme Court's decision, but they certainly never hoped for the wheels of destiny to turn in such a truly unfathomable manner.

The Brown vs. Board of Education decision was about the possibilities for equality among Blacks and Whites above anything else. It was about the possibility of freedom for most Blacks and the possibility of an interracial community for Blacks and Whites in segregated parts of the country, and particularly in the South. However, for strongly divided racial militant groups it was a day of great despair. In fact, for them this historical event was labeled "Black Monday" and many who protested the Supreme Court's decision also vowed that someone would certainly pay for the unprecedented ruling. White Citizen Councils were immediately armed, hoping to retaliate and to bring about an unsettling form of just-us. They were determined to form an alliance against Blacks and to do whatever was necessary to show African Americans that they were not required to observe or to follow any law that they determined was an unjust law, which of course was left up to their own racist interpretation.

In the years to immediately follow that decision, tensions built up in the South at an all time high. And throughout the country several African American leaders and martyrs would soon be assassinated as a direct result of this social climate of hate. Over and over again the individuals to lose their lives would change, but the issue would still be the same. An African American would stand up for their rights, not be willing to remain complacent with racial divides, or simply and unequivocally end up in the wrong place at the wrong time. Whatever the specific issues were, it was always assumed that our lives were worth risking and literally left hanging in the balance. As a direct result, the history and social fabric of American history was stained, and the heart of African Americans in this country was broken yet time and time again. In fact, one of the most significant events to occur shortly after the Supreme Court decision was the lynching of Emmett Till in 1955 when it became apparent that even an African American child would not be safe in the United States due to the quickly deteriorating race relations. And there were still countless others who lost their lives in the struggle for civil rights; there was Martin Luther King Jr., Medgar Evers, Malcolm X; all the way down from the famous to the little known. But with each life that was lost in the struggle, the spirit of African American people became a little more displaced in the United States, our social identity compromised and we were left with a huge gaping hole where the words of true leaders once echoed in our hearts."

—**E. Willa Simpson**

"Lynching was about the extraordinarily powerful, symbolic and quite literal control of the Black body. It was about hanging the Black body in space and suspending the upward mobility of both Black men and women. *It was about controlling the movement of the Black body . . . and symbolically lynching took on such a heavy weight because of its terrorizing implications and even deadening consequences in some sense of the Black freedom struggle because of the arbitrary violence to which Black people would be subjected to in lynching was an exemplification of the heart of White supremacy.* Its sub textural logic was made manifest. And what was also made manifest was that the Black body should be destroyed, contained; have a noose set around it and be suspended from the limbs of White supremacy. So not only was it heavily metaphoric, it was also quite literally about foregrounding some of the most vicious and evil meanings in the domination of Black culture and the violent manner in which White supremacy intended to control the Black body."

—Michael Eric Dyson

"During my childhood I remember of course the case of Emmett Till who was lynched in Mississippi. I can remember the case of the Martinsville Seven. There were a number of cases. And of course during the civil rights era, you have the three civil rights workers who were killed (James Chaney, Andrew Goodman and Michael Schwerner). Most recently James Byrd in Texas was dragged from the back of a pickup truck by White men, one of whom had served time in prison and had apparently been lured into the Aryan Brotherhood and had developed his extremist positions on race; his racist White supremacist ideas while he was in prison. So certainly when we talk about the relationship between lynching and ideology, lynching is the most extreme form of racism that expresses itself in many less dramatic ways; that expresses itself economically, that expresses itself in the educational system, that expresses itself in California with the passage of proposition 209 and the dismantling of affirmative action."

—Angela Davis

STRANGE FRUIT

The eyes of justice
are blinded by the rich,
but it don't bother itself
'bout the poor.
So I will probably
be swinging
from a magnolia tree
for darned sure.

REVOLUTION

What is a revolution to me?
A streets uprising
Burning trees
Desolate and full of grief
Injustice runs throughout the streets.

And Liberty's crown torn down by thieves
As freedom prevails on Judgment's Eve
As tears fall angrily and knees slowly to the ground
As a city repents forcefully and without sound.

THE BIG COMPROMISE

President Lincoln
freed the slave
split and divided
a small segment
of the land.
Thus, forty acres
and a mule
that day
would serve as fair
exchange
for the rape
and disillusionment
of what was called
three-fifths a man.

THE LYNCHING TREE

The north wind blows
a suspect breeze
through the tall, barren limbs
of the lynching tree.
There's a silence
hung in the air
that is as piercing
as stone.
This place may seem familiar
But it is not our home.
Resentment and bitterness
hung like leaves
on the once fertile limbs
of the lynching tree.
Where there was hope
There is now despair.
Where there was peace
death fills the air.
There was no justice
for those
whose lives were ended
tragically
in this God-awful place.
There is no justice
for the descendants
of former slaves
whose lives were ended
violently
and without cause.
When they took him away
in the midnight hour
where was the law?
A suspect wind blows

E. Willa Simpson

Over the brow of the man
that clings to his life
while hanging from the
once barren limbs
of the lynching tree . . .
But who cares
and who will see?

"The Lynching Tree represents a historical point of reference for people of African descent. It is that shared experience of bondage, in which our ancestors were tortured, humiliated and oppressed by their captors."

—E. Willa Simpson

MERCILESS

Weary faces ponder
the injustice of the street.
It is the only home they know.
And yet, they are doomed
to sit in judgment . . .

As tragedy awaits them
around dark corners,
and empty allies.
Deceivingly to mark
the existence of their days.

As propositions pass
like restitution
for their suffering.

"The death of Emmett Till was an extraordinarily galvanizing moment in the development of Black consciousness, as well as in the development of a social rebellion against White Supremacy and apartheid in the South. Initially of course, with his death which was one of the most heinous symbols of the desire of White America to contain and control Black mobility and an expression of the institutional mechanisms by which White America would maintain and preserve its hegemony; Emmett Till's death sparked a person like Rosa Parks who subsequently refused to give up her seat on a Montgomery bus as part of a well oiled machinery of resistance that had been built up in Montgomery, Alabama. It wasn't just a random act of social conscience, but rather the byproduct of an extraordinarily long legacy; a subconscious strategy to articulate Black freedom and equality. *But that was undeniably a galvanizing moment; that is the death of Emmett Till. Emmett Till after all represented the innocence of our Black future, the innocence of our Black youth. He represented the potential of our future cutoff, severed, drowned literally; beat, suffocated and drowned.* So the bloating of his body and his face, the heinous disfigurement that he endured as a result of this horrible crime was an unavoidable metaphor for how the future of Black youth was being challenged, subverted, undermined, destroyed, distorted by White supremacy and about how we must make a concerted effort to respond to not only the event itself, but also the legal structure that allowed it to stand without redress undeniably, as his mother Mamie Till Mobley spoke about it."

—Michael Eric Dyson

The fourteen year old youth who would later become known to the world as "Emmett Till," had allegedly been abducted by two White men while visiting relatives in the Mississippi Delta. The men forced their way into his Great Uncle, Moses Wright's home while demanding to take away the young boy who was immediately from Chicago. They wanted Emmett Till specifically because he had been accused of having wolf-whistled at the wife of Roy Bryant, one of his abductors. But despite the pleas of his Great Aunt and Uncle to take their money instead, the two men made off with Emmett Till into the dark of night; throwing him into the back of an old Chevrolet pickup truck as he pleaded for his life in vain. Emmett's body turned up three days later in the Tallahatchie River, with a cotton gin fan tied fatally around his neck with barbed wire and it is believed that his abductors had severely tortured the youth for several long hours leading up to his untimely death. Once his body was discovered, the state officials ordered the casket to remain shut, placing several seals on it in various locations, and insisted that there be a closed casket funeral. His body would later be released to the funeral home director, A. A. Rainer, but not before extended family members were forced to sign and promise that under no circumstances would his casket be opened. *However, after the body arrived home in Chicago, Emmett's courageous mother Mamie Till Mobley demanded that it be opened immediately . . . at all costs.* However, what she saw once they opened the casket was a terribly horrific scene.

—E. Willa Simpson

"His tongue was hanging down near his chin, one of his eyes was lying on his cheek, the other one was gone as if someone had taken a nut picker and picked it right out . . . *it was just gone.* The bridge of his nose looked like they had taken a hatchet and chopped the bridge of his nose. And while I'm looking at all of these things, by his mouth being open I could see that he only had three or four teeth left . . . and I paused to say what a pity; meaning those were some of the most beautiful teeth I had ever seen and for all of those teeth to be beaten out of him like that, it was just a gross thing to me. Then I went to look at his ear because I really had to figure out what that was or who that was. *I'm never going to say that I looked at him at once and said that's my child. I did not know what it was.*"

—Mamie Till Mobley
Mother of Emmett Till

UN-JUSTICE

The defensible
un-doings
of injustice.

"And somehow we continue to have unjust laws recorded on the books which are used disproportionately against African Americans, such as in the case of the '**Stand Your Ground Law in Florida**' which allowed Trayvon Martin, a fifteen year old unarmed Black youth to be brutally gunned down by a White neighborhood watch captain who deemed him "suspicious" by virtue of being an African American male, who was wearing a hoodie in an upscale gated community of Florida . . . on the wrong day; and also apparently at the wrong time."

—**E. Willa Simpson**

"I became involved with the Black Panther Party in the sixties, not too long after the party was founded. My motivation was to create a better world for Black people and all people who were racially oppressed by virtue of class. I did an enormous amount of work with the Black Panther Party, but I never became a part of the leadership structure of the Black Panther Party . . . *but I felt at the time that it was extremely important to be associated with the most radical, the most militant Black formation challenging police brutality, focusing also on economic issues and contesting capitalism.*"

—**Angela Davis**

"Emmett Till was one of many, many individuals who were lynched during the early civil rights movement due to the climate of racial bigotry and hate. In fact, during this era there were many eyewitnesses to such atrocities, particularly in the South. African Americans struggled to make sense out of this uncertain reality and to find whatever means they could to protect their children, and attempt to instill in them a fear of interacting amongst Whites. *However, despite the best intentions, time and time again; yet another child would fall victim to such a senseless, dreadful crime.*"

—**E. Willa Simpson**

"I've been asked about the role that Medgar Evers played during the Emmett Till trial; during the trial of Emmett Till's murderers. Medgar Evers along with Dr. T.R.M. Howard made it their business to go into the cornfields, into the local townships and to scout for people who had been eyewitnesses or knew something about what had happened; if they had heard the noise or knew about the character of the tormentors, the murderers. And one thing that Medgar Evers did . . . it was his responsibility to get Moses Wright (The Great Uncle of Emmett Till from whose home he had been abducted.) back and forth from the courtroom in one piece. *And I understand that he came upon the ingenious idea of smuggling him in a casket, from the courtroom to Memphis, and then it was his job to get him back to court the next morning."*

—Mamie Till Mobley
Mother of Emmett Till

THE FUNERAL

I laid my brother down to rest
Lord Jesus, did you see me?
Thought I would never breathe again
And that you had deceived me.

I cried for one year and some days.
I wonder, did you hear me?
I felt the world should stop
When he was gone.

I searched the souls of men
For many answers.
For he died so undeservedly,
With the speed of cancer.
And his body was left to bury
Along with the shattered pieces
Of my heart.

The saints sang songs of chariots
And kingdoms.
But I was his sister,
How could I leave him?
And how could he leave me
In this tired old bitter world
Without a song?

"They tell me that over 600,000 people passed by Emmett's casket and that one in five had to have assistance. They were falling out, they were fainting . . . *and they were screaming.* They were just doing everything. I had to have the body moved that Saturday morning. It arrived on a Friday evening, and by that Saturday morning I had to have it moved to 4021 S. State Street to the Robert's Temple Church of God in Christ because Mr. Rainer (the funeral home director) said, *"Ms. Mobley they're going to push my funeral establishment off of its foundation and there's no way that I can stop the crowd . . ."* and there wasn't. Mayor Daley had put I don't know how many policemen on duty trying to control the crowd that Friday evening; and the crowd was getting angry and began to threaten the White officers. So he had to pull the White officers and put all Black officers on the scene. *But they still didn't respond to them.* I asked them to help me find a place to stand outside of the funeral home. There were thousands of people outside that funeral home and they were pushing trying to get in and they were getting angry with one another if somebody closed up a space. And we found a place for me to stand in a window and I would talk to the crowd from that window and tell them, "All of you will get in, but please don't push. We don't want anybody to get hurt." Then they would ease the line up and stop the pushing. But this wouldn't last for very long. I had to keep repeating my message as long as I was there. *And when I got ready to go, I remember thinking, "Will that building be here when I get back in the morning?"* But thank God, everything was under enough control and they didn't push the building off of its mooring."

—Mamie Till Mobley
Mother of Emmett Till

"I have done some research on the role that rape accusations played in encouraging lynch mobs. Ida B. Wells of course was the most amazing activist and journalist who exposed the extent to which the invocation of rape charges was often enough to set a mob on a Black man regardless of whether there were any circumstances that had to do with any kind of sexual contact or sexual abuse. Now of course, it's important to be able to combine an awareness of the racist use of the rape charge with an understanding that the patriarchal structures have had a profound impact on the Black community as well. Therefore, we can't allow a campaign against the fraudulent rape charge to prevent us from taking on those men in our community who are responsible for abuse; sexual abuse against women. And I think that's still really hard, it's still really hard for people to be able to recognize how closely those are linked; and of course on another level this happened in relation to the Clarence Thomas case when there were those who insisted that he be made accountable for the kinds of harassment that Anita Hill suggested he was responsible for. But at the same time we need to point out that he was setup as a figure. *Well, one might say that as he sat there dealing with all of these charges, he sat against the background of all of these White men who more than likely were equally responsible for behavior that was just as bad or even worse than Thomas' behavior, but they were never called to answer.* So it's complicated and I think we need to play that kind of a balancing act if we're going to develop our consciousness today."

—**Angela Y. Davis**

"In recent years, we are now witnessing so many African American men formerly accused and convicted of sexual crimes against women being exonerated and proven innocent. Thanks to developments in technology and more specifically in the area of DNA evidence, the truth is finally coming out. And yet, how can we as a society even begin to repay these men for the many years that they have spent locked up behind bars; especially when so many of them were locked up for the greater and more significant part of their lives. Relationships have been devastated, integrity robbed, freedom denied, jobs no longer waiting for them and in some cases, even their sense of identity is lost. I mean . . . . how do you just pick up from that point and move on? And just imagine how many innocent men are still being wrongfully imprisoned to this very day due to that one particular era in our history alone. It's a sad reality for our nation and one that we're ashamed to address, although it's definitely been long overdue."

—**E. Willa Simpson**

IN MY SOLITUDE

Here I sit
bathing in tears
and casting out
demons.
Waiting for the sunrise
before the storm.
Wallowing in pity;
shameful that I am bothered;
and much too afraid
to part my feeble wings
and fly . . .

How is it
that you awaken me,
set roses
upon my table,
then let me live
to see them dwindle
before my sight?

And am I not
the ROSE?
Have I not watched
my own DEATH
a thousand times?

And can I be
complete
in the aftermath
of LOVING
when all that is left
of you and me
is I?

RWANDA BOY

A face like mine
Two black hands
Two black feet

Saddened tears
Deep brown eyes
A distant mind
A different peace

Impending fears
Transcending cries
A look of loss
Despair

A desperate thought
A faltered sigh
A tiny space
A lonesome stare

Hierarchy debate
Authoritarians vote
A second lost
His brother cries

A father executed
A mother's hunger
His sister calls out
His brother dies

He waits for Jesus
He sits and stares
In distant places.

LONELY HEART

I've known what it meant to be lonely.
But I've never known loneliness, like I know now.
I've known what it felt like to have my heart broken.
But I never knew the feeling of being broken hearted.

I've known of love and now love lost.
And it seems as though you have silently slipped AWAY.

And so, to the Black man that knows rivers . . .
I know you.

With passing days, I know and love you even more
My brother, dear heart.

A SILENT FRIEND

When it seems that everything around you
Just doesn't make sense
And the road that is less traveled
Waits eagerly there at your feet.

When all that is gold
Has turned into dust
And solely sorrow remains.

Remember that God can pull you up
If only you'll ask it, in Jesus name.

THE STRUGGLE

Take me to a place where I can be free
Where love prevails and evils cease
Where a drive-by is a whim that has no bearing
And brothers pass with As-Salaam-Alaikum and no idol staring.

Where females are not disrespected
Where I can live peacefully and not be killed
Where Black on Black don't refer to a crime
And it definitely don't refer to doing time.

Where statistics refer to a society that's united by love
And a sister don't have to fight so hard, just to come up.

FOOTSTEPS

Little Mecca
Touch my being,
Lead me to a land
Of old.

Pass down the secrets
Of our colorful
Forefathers.

Bring the distance
Of my yearning
To a close.

Find me a place
Where dreams are trimmed
With unity.

And there will be
No harsh division
Of the land.

Teach me the wisdom
Of the sweetness
Of equality . . .

And let our children
Walk these footsteps
Hand in Hand.

"The Black Panther Party played a major role in demonstrating that it was possible to assume a radical position in challenging the prevailing racism. Whereas many of us who were young at the time tended to see the civil rights movement as important, we were somewhat reluctant to believe that integration assimilation was the ultimate solution. So while it was important to fight for civil rights, we certainly believed that it was also important to fight for economic rights and to raise the issue of racism outside of the South, where it did not necessarily express itself in legalized segregation. So the Black Panther Party in doing its initial work in challenging the police department and challenging what they used to call the police occupation of our communities, sparked the imagination of people not only across the country and not only Black people; but all kinds of people all over the world. As a matter of fact, there was a Black Panther Party that was created in Israel. In Brazil a new Black consciousness began to develop. So it really is impossible to overestimate the global impact of the Black Panther Party. And at the same time, you're talking about a group of young people, some of whom were relatively inexperienced and who took great risks and embarked upon experiments that older people might have been reluctant to embrace. *So I mean . . . the point is that there were a lot of problems as well, there were a lot of mistakes; a lot of strategies that really didn't work. But what I think is the most important lesson for young people today is that precisely it is important to take risks, it is important to be bold and to imagine new strategies and to develop a new vision.* And that's what the Black Panther Party did, in spite of all of their faults; they certainly have to be celebrated for that new vision."

—Angela Y. Davis

"Now just as Emmett's death impacted the South, when we went to the trial reporters came from all over the world. They came from Australia, from most of the countries in Europe, the Asian countries, the island countries; they came to attend that trial. And when they were threatened by the local people in Sumner, Mississippi they were in shock."

—Mamie Till Mobley
Mother of Emmett Till

"The civil rights movement quickly spread across the globe as news broke out on the brutality involved in Emmett Till's tragic lynching and due to the horrifically cruel nature of the crime. The issue of lynching was no longer confined to just the United States, but our foreign allies' now eagerly awaited daily news reports and updates concerning the trial. Supporters of the movement were quickly growing in numbers and waited anxiously to see what America was truly made of. *People wondered how such a travesty of justice could occur anywhere in the United States, even if it was the Mississippi Delta.* There were so many long overdue questions, but not merely enough answers."

—E. Willa Simpson

REMEMBERING BILLIE

"Although few recognized her as such during the time of her brief existence, famed jazz legend Billie Holiday was also a civil rights leader of sorts. Her infamous and heart wrenching classic entitled "*Strange Fruit*" was her own personification of the social ravages and subhuman treatment of African Americans through both the illogical and irrational psychological processes involved in lynching. *Billie's first performances of this song were presented before almost all white audiences and met with utter shock and extreme disapproval among less liberal audience members. However, in spite of the initial unpopularity of the song, Billie persevered and continued to sing it, even as painful as this experience must have been for her and those who could identify with her pain.* The legendary classic would prove its enduring significance as it eventually brought audience members down to their knees and also became a signature hit of the belated songstress crowned by many as "Lady Day." Her work and contributions to the struggle were essential in opening up critical dialogue on the social consequences and little talked about injustices surrounding the culture and history of lynching."

—E. Willa Simpson

BILLIE'S MIDNIGHT JAM

Pouting lips
Sweet melodies
Tapping toes
Jazzy tunes

Kick back baby
Do that cha cha
And sing them awesome
Midnight blues!

Dedicated to the late Billie Holiday.

THE TRUMPET PLAYER

It was i
that breathed love
into his nostrils
when my lips met
with his.

But what a shame . . .
he didn't feel it.

My heart danced
naively
to the rhythm
of a drum.

SWING LOW

Sometime in thought
I wish that I
Could jump across
The wall of heaven
Into a bed
Filled with my sorrow

And drown
Amongst
My tears.

"I think that it is important for people to remember Emmett Till because it's a part of history, part of the world shaping and a part of the United States civil rights movement. It's a part of things that happened that people should know about in the history of the world and how things really evolved and what was done; even if it was right or wrong. Because that's what history is about and Emmett Till will always be history."

—Howard Bingham
Producer of Motion Picture Film "Ali"

"Why do I think Emmett's death was significant . . . ? Well, in a vision that the Lord showed me the Wednesday that we received news that he was dead, the Lord appeared to me and He said that Emmett was not mine, that I should be thankful for the length of time that he did spend with me. And he began to compare Emmett with his son, Jesus. He said, "My son Jesus came here and became sin." He said, "The sins of the world were put on my son, and He came here that men might have a choice between eternal life and eternal damnation. And my son Emmett came here and gave his life so that men would see how ugly race hatred is and that men would be able to have freedom here on Earth. And now Mamie . . . . there's a job for you to do." And when this was said to me, I rejected it. I thought I'd done enough. I'd given my only child; my mother's only grandchild, my father's only grandson. I had no sisters and no brothers, so where am I going to pour out all of this love; only first cousins left. *And it looks like the Lord kind of ignored me and kept on with what he wanted to say. But he let me know that Emmett became race hatred so man could experience how ugly, how dangerous, how frightening race hatred really is.* And the comparison with his son Jesus . . . . that struck a cord with me. And later I went back and examined that because I'm used to seeing Jesus with a crown of thorns. I'm accustomed to seeing Him with a little blood trickling down and yet my Bible tells me that his visage was scarred as no other man's. And I said . . . then Jesus did not look like that picture I have seen. If He looked worse than Emmett looks, then He must have had a terrific encounter with his tormentors because they beat him all night long and led Him from judgment hall to judgment hall. And Emmett, they only beat him about six hours and God knows that was long enough because in the course of this beating one of them according to an eyewitness took an axe and came down the top of his head . . . . and that's why the ear was gone when I looked for it, and that's why I could see from the temple area, all the way to daylight on the other side. *And I wondered was it necessary to put that bullet in his brain, but yes it was.* If Emmett had not suffered what he suffered, the world would still be doing a Rip Van Winkle. We would yet be sleeping; Mississippi would yet be lynching to her hearts content, other people would yet be riding segregated buses and the laws of the land would have never changed. After Emmett died, there was so much unrest in Alabama until when Rosa Parks was asked to give up her

seat, she refused. She said she was angry and her soul was tired; not her feet. She said, 'I was tired of being abused the way I was.' And she took a chance on her life because she was lashing out on what happened to that little boy. And we know what happened there. The bus boycott lasted over a year; I think 382 days and then the federal government changed the laws."

—Mamie Till Mobley
Mother of Emmett Till

"Well certainly there is a consciousness of the traumatic impact of lynching on Black communities from the aftermath of the civil war on. When James Byrd for example in Texas is dragged by White supremacists driving a pickup truck, that immediately evokes many of the repressed feelings about the historical impact of lynching. And that's something that I think we have to figure out how to deal with. *Haile Gerima in his film "Sankofa" argued that he made this film because Black people still have not been able to start the process of healing in relation to slavery and that it is important to think about and acknowledge and talk about those horrors in our history as opposed to shrouding them with silence; forgetting about them and not wanting to talk about them.* I know when I was a child, my grandmother would rarely talk about her growing up years and I think in many Black families there was a tendency to sort of relegate bad things to the past and to feel that if we just don't talk about them, they'll go away. But of course, if you don't talk about them, they fester and become more painful. And therefore it is time to start acknowledging them."

—Angela Y. Davis

"Unfortunately, I can remember that even for my own Grandmother, that she too had a lot of trouble discussing such tragic events from the past. It was almost like she sensed that at anytime the course of history could change yet again; possibly even for the worse. And so the older generation tended to pray a lot, treat each day as a gift and do their best to move forward and make something out of whatever they did or did not have. I can only thank God that when she passed on from this Earth that the heavy weight from such issues was far removed from her heart; but should we have to wait until death or the conformity of the grave?"

—E. Willa Simpson

STATISTICS SAY

What do today's
Statistics say?
Do they apply
To I?

Inherently cruel
Heathenistic rule
A paganistic
Republican
Rise

And color shades
Blind open eyes
To conclude
What is preconceived?

What will today's
Statistics say
And will they apply
To me?

FREEDOM RIDE

Democracy
is just an illusion
until you set my people
free.

"Well I guess one of the things I would say is that the civil rights movement was never extended to prisoners and the institution of the prison. So the same kinds of issues that were taken on in the 1950's and 1960's by the civil rights movement really need to be taken on in relation to the two million people who are behind bars today and their political freedom. *You know, first of all I guess I should point out that the prison historically was designed not to repress every aspect of a person's liberties and rights, but basically only to deprive that person of his or her freedom. It was not designed to eradicate all civil rights, all human rights, but that is what it has become. It's become an institution that is used disproportionately against people of color; disproportionately against Black people.* Over one million of the two million prisoners today are Black and increasing numbers of them have lost; have permanently lost their right to participate in the political life of our society. *In Alabama, one third of all Black men who were eligible to vote have become permanently disenfranchised by virtue of having been in prison and then no one considers that increasing numbers of people are going to prison because prison has become that institution which is presented as the default solution to every major social problem that we have.* It is a rather scary situation. But I do think that the legacy of the civil rights movement ought to be brought to bear in relation to a movement for the rights of prisoners."

—Angela Y. Davis

I AM MOVED

Frequently I listen
to my conscience
and I am moved
to feel compassion deep within . . .

For others without voice,
without position.
For those without status,
without money.
For those that are hungry
and are needy
for what only I have
to give.

For the satisfied
do not appreciate,
taking my kindness
without embracing
leaving my heart empty
like a vase
without a rose.

But thank God
that there is someone
who in their longing
seeks to find me
and when they do
I am very deeply . . .
Moved.

DEAREST CORRETTA

There will come a time
When your smile
Won't seem so dim.
Those dark brown eyes
Won't hang so low.
Yes Lord,
There'll come a time.

When all shall be new
And the voices
Of yester-year
Shall prevail
As an eternal sunrise
Lifting the prayers
Of loved ones
Far above
The illusive shadow
Of the moon.

And your tears
Are NOT forgotten.
The road you've paved
We FREQUENTLY travel.
Your sacrifices
Are cherished DEEPLY
Within my soul.

Be patient sister . . .
For I am sure
Our time will come.

Dedicated to our beloved Corretta Scott King.

CONGRESSIONAL PROPAGANDA

Freedom
Is the silver tinsel
On somebody else's
Christmas tree.
So long as everybody
—ain't free.

"I was actually quite young in 1955 when the Montgomery Bus Boycott was organized. I was eleven years old at that time, so I was aware of what was going on. I felt solidarity, but I wasn't directly involved. Later when I went to high school in New York, I did become actively involved in a number of organizations that supported the work that was happening in the South. When I was fifteen years old, I became involved in a group that picketed Woolworth's every Saturday morning to challenge its discriminatory treatment of Black people in the South. I did that kind of thing, marches and so forth from the time that I was about fourteen or fifteen. And I was one of many, many people; one of hundreds of thousands of people who wanted to see the world change at that time."

—Angela Y. Davis

"One of the great figures in the early civil rights movement was of course, Ida B. Wells. She was an extraordinary woman in many ways; a journalist, public intellectual to be sure by virtue of her strong expression and identity as a woman; and certainly a feminist in the best sense of the word. She was an extraordinarily important figure who seized on this issue of lynching. And at the heart of lynching was the expression of the repudiation of the erotic and sexual identities of Black men in particular, but also the containment and curtailment of the mobility of African people in general in America."

—Michael Eric Dyson

ESSENCES OF BLACKNESS

I am today's black woman
Intelligent
Dark and beautiful
Sho'nough fine

Dedicated to my people
To this prideful struggle
Our hands devise

Looking forward to tomorrow
And trying hard
To find solutions

Questions of life and love
Racial and moral
I bear the cross
Of resolution.

I am today's . . .
Black woman.

"Well, of course a lot of Black people who have had the status of important figures in our history and leaders have been assassinated. I think about Dr. Martin Luther King Jr., I think about Medgar Evers, I think about Malcolm X of course. *And I guess I would say that we don't need anymore martyrs and that it was not their assassination that was responsible for their status, it was the work that they did when they were alive.* And I think that is what we must insist upon and that is the message that young people should be willing to listen to. And much of the work that they did was not glamorous work. It was organizing work. And unfortunately in many instances, many of the Black men who we acknowledged as leaders were only able to ascend to that status because of the work that Black women did. And that is the work that rarely gets acknowledged. I always say that organizing is the housework of the movement and that's the work that so many women performed and those women to this day . . . most of them still have no names."

—Angela Y. Davis

FOR OUR BELOVED MAKAVELI:

Who's going to help us now?
Who's going to insist that we are heard?
Who's qualified to be our voice?
Who's going to ride big brother's back?
Who's willing to become the poster child for injustice?
Who's going to be my bridge over many troubled waters?
Who's going to further our cause?
Who's willing to stand up and to challenge the laws?
Who's going to speak up for us now?
Who's going to save the Black man now?

Dedicated to Tupac and Afeni Shakur.

REMEMBERING TUPAC

"Tupac Shakur was one of the most critical and influential figures in the hip-hop movement who also had deep roots in the Black Panther Party; both of his parents having been deeply associated with this critical period in American history. He was raised by a single mom "Afeni Shakur" and would live on to transcend many aspects of the poverty that had at one time devastated his family life. However, out of his own attempts to be down with his people and relate to the impoverished communities of Black and Brown, combined with his affiliations to "thug life" characters, this pivotal figure in American history would eventually be gunned down by his less enlightened counterparts. However, his spirit and the true intentions of his work will live on for many centuries to come. Young people and educators across the globe will continue to refer to his work and writings for the core of what young Black America, the impoverished and the disenfranchised Black male is truly attempting to express through his existence, purpose, unapologetic dissertation and hypnotic rhyme. His compelling and thoughtful lyrics, "Dear Mama" will ring in the hearts of single Black mothers for many years to come and on their worst days they will continue to play his song and remember that we are much greater than our circumstances and victors in this life; not merely victims of the struggle. We will also remember his lyrics for "Brenda's Got a Baby" as we continue to dialogue on the issue of teenage pregnancy which has now reached epidemic proportions in the United States. His message was not so much about the glorification of the Gang or Thug life, as it was about creating a new dialogue to address the injustices and social ills of the "ghetto."

—E. Willa Simpson

"Tupac was an extraordinary manifestation of the conflicted terrain involving political recognition of the forces of social stasis and destabilization on the one hand; social stasis drawn from Black political revolutionary rhetoric to say that this is what we need to survive and this is who we are, and that we must love one another. And social destabilization in the sense of that fallout from the inability of revolutionary rhetoric first of all to move Black people and Brown people forward. And secondly, to provide enough space for these folk to survive long enough to regroup in the face of the forces of gentrification. And thirdly, just the outright distance between the progressive Black bushwah culture on the one hand and the working poor and the persistent poor on the other. Tupac was representative of the conflicted and moral ambitions and the social legacies of the struggle against White supremacy; both from above, that is from Black progressive political activity. And from below; meaning from the underground economy of which gangster rap and his version of thug rap are the most powerful symbols within the hip-hop culture."

—Michael Eric Dyson

"Now what I am saddened about is that along with this new freedom has come a reign of terror, Black on Black. Our children have been introduced to things that they shouldn't even know exist, such as drugs and so many other things that we worry about, gang relationships and so forth. But we know . . . . we know that there is nothing too hard for God. We know that this is going to pass, but it is up to us as parents, as educators and as adults to mentor these children to the utmost."

—Mamie Till Mobley
Mother of Emmett Till

WAKE UP

Brothers are out there on the corner
Trying hard to make a dollar
They call a gang their family
For they've replaced the role
Of their fathers.

Leaving babies, broken hearts
And his regrets, along the way.
Well, get ready for a great uprising.
Your sisters need you here today.
The system's taking all our rights!
Three strikes you're out, they say.
As though our lives held no great importance.
He is consumed by the digits
That he so deceptively loves to play.

Yet, what happened to "Black Unity?"
And we shall overcome?
It seems that freedom is not cheap
And justice not been done.

And so we thought the battle won.
Depended upon a non-inclusive Constitution
And diligently waited for Freedom's ring
As our taxes bought more and more
Of these racist institutions.

And thus began the story
Of the "New World Order Slavery."
I perceive the time to be waiting eagerly at hand.
History will only repeat itself
We have learned through past experiences.
And we're in no position today
To be dealing with, the MAN.

We must stand and take another look
Breakdown the codes of this foundation.
Seek wisdom throughout these last days
And not be broke down by a nation.

Brothers you got to . . .
WAKE UP!

"First of all, the high rates of incarceration now have little to do with any increase in the rate of crime. *As a matter of fact, the crime rates have been steadily declining over the last years, while the incarceration rates have been steadily rising.* I think that imprisonment has become far too profitable; that many more institutions, agencies, companies and corporations have a stake in an expanding prison population because it's become profitable in many ways. *Punishment has become an industry, so of course it's important to find the bodies to punish.* Whereas it used to be that drugs, particularly drugs like marijuana would not result in a long sentence for the convicted person. Now we have these mandatory minimum sentences, we have truth in sentencing laws so that not only are more people going to prison, but people are spending longer periods of time behind walls. And if we don't do something about this, the Black community is certainly going to suffer enormously."

—Angela Y. Davis

HEAVY

I.

When Black is Black
And trouble seems so far away
It is death that lurks behind life's hidden doors.

And it is because we are so eager
To pretend that we do not see
That it consistently continues to beg
For even more.

More lives to claim
From a struggle not yet acknowledged
That today many claim its existence, not to be.

But this accusation, as well as the belief in alone
Breeds death to become stronger
And it therefore becomes our bleak and sullen, dark reality.

II.

Stop!!!
You must take heed, my brother
For this warning comes
With so very little time

For the bloodshed of our race
Grows deeper and deeper
And it seems that all love has been cast down
Aside.

III.

From one brother to another
I will have no love for you
Because I feel that you have no love for me.

You see it's all about coming up
And despite the fact that you are my brother
I'll take your life even quicker
Than your mere anticipation to blink.

IV.

Said I sold my soul
To the devil one day
And I put that on the red, white and the blue.

And now I'm taking my brothers out
Over the same gang colors
They said represented equal opportunities for me
And also for you.

Well, there'll be no opportunities
For you, my brother
For I feel that there have been no opportunities
For me.

And so now I'm stimulated to the point of pure destruction
Over nothing but the simplistic pretext of a color
As I fight to pursue the ignorance of another man's
Pathologically destructive dream.

V.

Most people believe my struggle
To be an issue of pride
But this gang has become the only family that I know.

And so now I'm straight bangin'
And selling drugs on the side
Wondering if tomorrow will ever free my troubled soul.

VI.

Help me, my brothers
Though it seems like I have no feelings
My existence is comprised of the anger and bitterness
I feel within.

And I keep asking myself
Where was my family when I needed them
And so now I'm fighting hard to stop these angry tears
For which it seems, there is no END.

VII.

Young brothers coming up
Is giving me much respect
And I just want to tell them don't trip
Cause this life on the streets, it ain't even about no game.

But for the first time in my life
Brothers is looking up to me
And I know if I be tellin' them the truth
The older brothers' respect for me ain't goin' never be the same.

It took time to earn this title
As well as the respect that I have now
But I have to kick back and remember
Time is also running out for me.

I been out here tripping in the streets
Doing drive-by's like it ain't nothing
Seeking destruction
And destroying my black brothers' illusive peace.

VIII.

Gangster, Gangster
Why are you so steadily killing
Taking your own brothers lives in ignorance
And in vain.

Don't you realize that life here in the ghetto is short
And just as sure as homicide is the number one killer
Of young Black men
In eternity
Your soul will most definitely remain.

IX.

Now don't go tripping out on me
Thinking that I'm coming down like rain
For you know that your sista'
She has much love for you.

But I want you to recognize
The mass manipulation
That's been killing off our brothers.
The mere essence of the colors
The red, white and the blue.
And let my sisters scream out
From the rooftops of Little Armageddon
That we have seen enough killing in our streets
Today.

And you must acknowledge death
To be the one ailment in life
Of which there is no ability to perceive
Even the slightest element of change.

Now I am trying hard to understand you
And to understand the pain that you are feeling
But I will not allow you to be destroyed
In vain.

You got the Mothers out here crying
You got the Daddies feeling helpless
But I say to you my brother
Something has got to give or change.

X.

And as a message to the Nation
While you're steadily calling for gang truces
It looks a little like everybody's set tripping
If you ask me.

Yeah
And true enough, he got his gang rags
And y'all, them damn colors!
And you better believe it ain't no justice out here
On these streets.

Take Heed.

"In the aftermath of the Brown vs. Board of Education decision, tensions between Blacks and Whites in the South reached an all time high. Angry white southerners were faced with the reality of school integration and feared that their precious White daughters would soon be going to school alongside African American youth. *A fourteen year old Black boy named Emmett Till visited the Deep South in the aftermath of the Supreme Court decision. And as a result of the racially chaotic atmosphere, several individuals were brutally lynched within a short period of time, but the most brutal of all was the lynching of . . . Emmett Louis Till."*

—E. Willa Simpson

"He was not really aware of the morays of the South and even though I tried my best to prepare him for going down South, I guess there was just no way that I could. I didn't have enough time to really get it into his head; the dangers of talking to and among White folks. I just had not been able to really get that into his head. *But what had happened was so trivial, that even had I been there on the scene, I would not have thought anything about it.*"

—Mamie Till Mobley
Mother of Emmett Till

"The lynching of Emmett Till, perhaps because Emmett Till came from the North; from Chicago, was one of the most publicized moments in the history of relations between Black and White people at that time . . . *for many people the case of Emmett Till marks a moment of awareness. In French you would say "extreme de conscience," a moment of coming to consciousness in a very intense way about the need to bring about social change."*

—Angela Y. Davis

"Unfortunately, we as Black people do not recap our history. We say don't talk about slavery times. We don't talk about the landlords who stole the money from the sharecroppers. They would work a team of thirteen strong from one part of the year to the other and when they went to settle up, the sharecropper's paper might say he'd made $1,500.00 that year. But the Master would say, "Well John, you've done pretty good . . . . you only owe me $250.00." So there was no way to actually make a living on the farm. The person who owned the farm; they were riding in big cars, wearing good clothes, and they had money to burn. But the poor sharecropper couldn't even buy his children apples for Christmas. If they got a few shoes and some yard goods, that was just about all they could afford. And when he started his farm again in the spring, he had to go back to the landowner and get all of his seeds on credit because he had no money left. *Now the Jewish people will not let us forget the Holocaust. If they had not filmed it, if they had not written about, had they not come on the air very often talking about it; we would begin to doubt if it had happened . . . but how can they deny it when 50,000 survivors have recorded their story and we can see and hear what happened to those poor people.* What about the Swiss Banks that folded on their money, wouldn't let the survivors know that they had money and took it for themselves. Right now they're having to pay it back. But what about us as Black people? We want to keep it a secret, we're ashamed that we're Black, we're ashamed that we were slaves; we're just full of shame. And until we learn to focus on our past history and to teach our children how to deal with it properly, then we're always going to be subject to the same kind of thing. In fact, we can't help but to think about James Byrd Jr. who was so brutally dragged to his death in Jasper, Texas. We cannot forget so many of our young people even here in Chicago who have crossed a certain racial barrier and been beaten within an inch of their lives. We cannot forget and must not forget the tragedy that happened in California with Rodney King. We have got to keep talking about it; we've got to keep dealing with it."

—Mamie Till Mobley
Mother of Emmett Till

YOUNG LITTLE EMMETT TILL

Little Emmett Till took a train ride to the Mississippi Delta, hoping to visit with his young cousins.

They innocently decided to take a trip to the "Bryant's Store," located in town.

Upon their arrival, the children dared Emmett to go into the store and say hello to an unsuspecting White storekeeper.

A crowd of curious youngsters frantically gathered all around.

Word says that Emmett Till wolf-whistled back to the woman just as he turned to leave . . .

But what did little Emmett Till possibly know about racism?

How could he understand that for this, his life he'd pay?

The children ran off eagerly, with a burst of excitement and vowed to keep the incident quiet. But the lynch mob quickly gathered, for Young Emmett's death, they would not delay.

The mob demanded to take away this young boy who was immediately from Chicago.

His Great Aunt wouldn't allow it and she tried to protect Little Emmett as best as she could.

All of the sudden, they struck his aunt on the side of her head, as his Uncle pleaded with them, in such great horror. And those angry white men took away Little Emmett deep off into the woods.

Days later they received the final word from cousin, Curtis.

Emmett's body was retrieved among the depths of the Tallahatchie River.

A cotton gin tied fatally around his neck with barbed wire.

This was the death; these white men said they chose for a nigger.

The town made a futile attempt to bury Little Emmett without his mother's permission.

His mother faced a great struggle, for young Emmett's funeral to be delayed.

And as she proceeded to stop this deceitful, suspicious, malicious burial,

What she found in little Emmett's casket caused her alarming shock and extreme dismay.

His body was disfigured beyond the point of recognition.

One eye gouged out and a bullet lodged deeply into his skull.

His forehead was crushed and miscellaneous parts were severed.

I suppose little Emmett cried until his weeping became a soft and bittersweet lull.

Mama Till declared the whole world to see little Emmett's body.
She declared the whole world to grieve and acknowledge little Emmett's pain.
Who can conceive this hateful mutilation of a precious little Black child's body?
Who can conceive this mother's loss of a child in such great vain?

And thus went down in history, the story of little Emmett.
In nineteen fifty-five, he was no exception to the Mississippi rule.
At the age of fourteen, this little Black boy's life was over.

And I cannot conceive how a gathering of men could be so cruel.

And thus went the story . . .
Of young, little Emmett Till.

This poem is based on the lynching of Emmett Till, a fourteen year old Black youth who was brutally lynched for being accused of wolf-whistling at a White woman.

FOR MAMA'S LITTLE BABY . . .

I didn't expect you'd leave me
so soon.
I didn't think
you'd ever part your wings
and fly.
What am I going to do now
with my life?
You were mama's little baby.
But why did you have to fly
away from me
so soon?

You once fluttered
in my stomach
like tiny butterflies
flapping wings
and preparing for
their very first flight.
You nestled in a place
So deep
That even I could not
resist you.
You were love
in its purest state.
You were the image
of our creator
and of the Divine.
You were the living image
of our Most High.
But why did you have
to fly away from me . . .
so soon?

Leaving me
beset with gloom.
and the choir sang . . .
I'll fly away
oh Glory,
I'll fly away . . .
but when will I ever see you again?
Will your tiny little footprints
ever touch the bottom
of my empty womb
again?
Will I ever be whole again?

How shall I ever fill up
this huge gapping hole
in my heart
again?
What will be my substitute
for love?
Will I ever get to see you dancing
with the angels
Or jumping over a cloud.
Will I ever get to see you smile
at me . . .
for the very first time?
Will I ever get to hold you
in my arms
and tell you that I love you
for the very first time?
Will I ever get to catch
a glimpse of you
sleeping peacefully
and know . . .
that you are close enough
to reach out and touch you.
How will I ever know
the sweet sound of your voice?

E. Willa Simpson

Will I ever be the same again?
Will I ever find my way again?
How can I ever truly be free again
without my baby's love?

Dedicated to Mamie Till Mobley, mother of Emmett Till.

"We got him to the station, we could hear the train blowing and Emmett was beginning to run up the steps and I said, "Bo, you didn't kiss me. How do I know I'll ever see you again? And it stopped him in his tracks and he turned around and said, *"Ah . . . Mama,"* like he was scolding me for saying that. But he ran back and gave me that kiss."

—Mamie Till Mobley
Mother of Emmett Till

"Well, I would say unfortunately there was a time when such tragic deaths were relatively routine, which isn't to say that we weren't all horrendously affected by the killings of you know . . . for example, the three girls who were dynamited to death at the Sixteenth Street Baptist Church; Carole Robinson, Addie Mae Collins and Cynthia Wesley. And those deaths had an immeasurable impact on the community, and on the families. *I was actually quite happy that Spike Lee decided to do a documentary called "The Three Little Girls" because some of that could be shared with the rest of us.* But I guess I've always felt that the best way to respond to those tragedies is to guarantee that the legacy of the person killed lives on, to keep that persons memory alive just as we try to keep the memories of Carole and Addie Mae and Cynthia alive; we try to keep the memories of Dr. Martin Luther King Jr. alive. *Not so much by doing what they did, but by building on their work, by standing on their shoulders.*"

—Angela Y. Davis

"The murder of Emmett Till took place in Money, Mississippi. It was a small village in the county of Tallahatchie, Mississippi; which was thirty five miles southeast of Clarksdale Mississippi. And the trial took place at Sumner, Mississippi; about fifteen miles on the Northeast side of Clarksdale, Mississippi."

—Ernest Whithers
Photojournalist covering the trial of Emmett Till's accused murderers.

"There were NAACP personnel from the South who attended the trial and sympathized with me and tried to help me to keep up my courage. My spirit was pretty well demolished, but they helped me to understand that in spite of the overwhelming evidence, that you may or may not get the right verdict. The people might turn out not guilty. When the trial was over, the evidence was so overwhelming until even a baby jury could have brought in a verdict of guilty. But when the jury retired, my spirit told me that we should retire. *I noticed that the people around the walls were quietly going out the back doors; the black people.* And that was significant to me. Why would they be leaving if they were expecting a triumphant verdict? When I told the people at our table that we should go, I remember they protested, "What . . . and miss the verdict?" I said, "This is one you're going to want to miss. The verdict is not guilty and when it comes in, the farther we are from here, the better off we're going to be." About forty-five minutes out of Sumner, Mississippi the jury foreman came to the microphone and said, "We the jury find the defendants not guilty." *And I'm telling you; you would've thought that the Yankees had won the pennant in New York City or the Bulls had won the basketball tournament in Chicago, Illinois. People went crazy. It was as if, okay . . . business as usual; it's open season on Negroes now.*"

—**Mamie Till Mobley**
Mother of Emmett Till

"*It was apparent that it was going to be a kangaroo court; hoping for justice, but expecting injustice.* And unfortunately we can tie that Emmett Till situation symbolically to the death of the young man in Cincinnati where recently a White judge dismissed the case against a policeman. And in hundreds of cases across this nation . . . *young Black men in particular*; black people are subjected to the tyrannical forces of police authority and then we are expected as Black people to somehow overlook such a heinous crime against our humanity or to pretend that it is part and parcel of the legal system, and we should accept that verdict as just. So Emmett Till was a reminder of the depths to which our bodies would be thrust and the even lower depth to which White people would sink to control and contain and to somehow corral the Black body; to cut it off from its nurturing source and root and to leave it defenseless in the face of the arbitrary violence that was manifest in apartheid and in White supremacy. *So it galvanized Rosa Parks and by galvanizing Rosa Parks, it galvanized the Montgomery Bus Boycott; and in galvanizing the Montgomery Bus Boycott, it galvanized Black masses around the country and in galvanizing Black masses around the country, it lead to the most extraordinary manifestation of the Black will to be free.* That was certainly witnessed in the twentieth century and arguably in our own history here in America. So that one single event setoff a chain of events that eventuated in the explosion of Black freedom struggles throughout this nation and symbolized the brutality and the utter horror of the White Supremacist logic that it could offend and that it could hurt, that it could kill, and that it could maim an innocent Black boy."

—Michael Eric Dyson

"The two men accused of the brutal lynching of Emmett Till; J.W. Milam and Roy Bryant were found not guilty only a few short hours after jury deliberations began. This news especially devastated the mother of the fourteen year old victim, Mamie Till Mobley. Then insult was added to injury when the accused killers confessed to the crime shortly thereafter in a nationally renowned news publication entitled, "Look Magazine."

—E. Willa Simpson

"It was a separate South. It was like a grossly separate America. A separate America being you know, which is far different. We live with a sense of separatism today all over, but it's by choice you know; we're a different people. You can't regulate the desires of another person to be in the presence of other ethnics. But it was more separate then because people lived separated by law. We went to separate schools, we lived in separate neighborhoods and we were of a different connectional imagery. *We were of the African American descendant and they were White.*"

—Ernest Whithers
Famed Photojournalist who covered the Emmett Till trial of 1955.

"It's actually very difficult to make a comparison between the overall consciousness of this society in say the late sixties and today. What I can say, is that without wanting to be nostalgic, that many people felt that their lives were much more directly affected by the political issues of the day; both those who were on the left, and those who were on the right. People I guess felt more directly implicated in the politics of the time. And that was both good and bad. It was good in the sense that it was perhaps easier to do the kind of organizing many of us did in the late sixties. It was not good in the sense that there was a much more simplistic understanding of politics. So that it really was usually about what side you were on. Today of course we recognize that we cannot draw a straight line and put all of those who represent the future on one side of the line and all of those who represent a kind of retrogressive reactionary position on the other side. It's much more complicated now. And anti-racist consciousness no longer works in the way it used to because we now recognize that it's also about gender and it's also about class; it's also about sexuality. So now our awareness is much more complex and those who are doing the activist work have to address a whole range of issues which people hadn't even begun to imagine at that time."

—Angela Y. Davis

"The lynching and murder of Emmett Till had affected a lot of people. And as you see, it had affected "Ali." As a matter of fact, there was a reference to it at the start of the "Ali" film that was just finished. It had opened with a little Black kid who was Ali getting on the bus and there was a gentleman at the time who was reading the newspaper and Ali looked over at the newspaper and you know, was wondering and then the guy turned (*The newspaper headlined the murder of Emmett Till*). It affected a lot of people, a lot of civil rights people. And even today, things are brought up about Emmett Till. Emmett Till will live on forever."

—Howard Bingham
*Producer of Motion Picture Film "Ali"

"*The penitentiary system in this country, the prison system was established as a tool that incorporated class domination as a strategy that incorporated racism.* As a matter of fact, the development of the system was given a special impetus at the end of the civil war when Black people were freed in the South. An institution which had been primarily a White institution became almost overnight a majority Black institution. So the prisons particularly in the South, but not exclusively in the South became a means by which to control free Black labor. *And that foreshadowed . . . it seems to me, the current period of the prison industrial complex.* Black labor was used as a source of profit in the nineteenth century in the aftermath of slavery. Black convict labor is now used as a source of profit within the framework of the prison industrial complex. But today of course punishment itself is far more profitable than it ever was before. With corporations that provide us with things that we use in our daily lives being implicated in one way or another in providing services for this expanded prison system or using prison labor as a source of super profits."

—Angela Y. Davis

"African Americans have learned to grin and bear the many disappointments that this life would bring simply as a result of being Black in America. After the conclusion of World War II, countless African American Soldiers returned home only to find that they still were not accepted in the United States, nor were they treated with any true sense of dignity, and many could not even find decent jobs to take care of themselves or their families."

—E. Willa Simpson

AUNT RHODA DALE

Her eyes
are filled with the gloom
of too many yesterdays
gone by
shooshing dandelions
in a field of gray.

IF MY LABOUR BE IN VAIN

And although the sun shine on me
In the brightness of a day
She don't really know me
She don't begin to know my heart.

And though she desperately will follow
My every waking footstep
She don't even seem concerned
To care to stop and ask,
My name.

She warms my heart
As she leaves tomorrow
On the fragile moments
Of my lasting breaths

But does she give in to question
The pain within my soul
Or nonetheless
How deeply I be
Consumed.

For as soon as I trust her
The night sneaks upon me
And she is gone
And I
Alone.

And I fall asleep
With thoughts of regretfulness
And promises
I know
I cannot keep.

And although my dreams sometime bring comfort
To a lonely soul that knows so little of true justice
It be seeming nothing much makes sense to me
Anymore.

For every time I think I understand my life
It changes reflectively
With the insecurity of time.

And every time I think that I am loved
The visions fade
Away.

Because it is love that is the distance
Of tiny hands, too short; to reach
Therefore, I am not one
Therefore, I am not complete
If my labor be
In vain.

"Well, I think that it's important to learn from the past, but I never imagined what things would have been like had I approached matters differently because today I know what I know in large part because of what I did in the past. And of course, in many instances we made mistakes. But we learned from those mistakes. And it's not possible to go back and rectify them. It is important however to learn from those errors and not repeat them in the future. So I don't have any regrets. *I really don't have any regrets and I don't think about what I would do differently. I think about what we can do now, based on what we know . . . which is in turn based on you know, what we've done in the past.* I think that's the connection. And that's why it's so important to have intergenerational relationships among activists, for older people to talk to younger people; not to tell them what to do and which way to go, but to share with them experiences so they're not doomed to repeat the errors of the past and so that they can move forward with a fresh and new vision."

—**Angela Y. Davis**

"For forty-four years I have dealt with this. I thought that within a given amount of time that the memories would fade. But they are as alive today, as they were yesterday. I am constantly being called upon . . . when a tragedy happens; my phone is going to ring in Chicago. *I'm going to be asked how do you feel about this, or does this remind you of your son? So if I wanted to forget, there would be no way.* I am sure that a minimum of three calls a week come in here and these conversations can go on for three and four hours. I can hear the person on the other end of the phone crying. *And that's one of the things the Lord said to me is that the world will always cry for Emmett Till.* I am just asking that I will be able to continue to carry the message; that I will live the kind of life that will make me the kind of messenger that I should be. Because as long as I'm telling the truth and as long as I'm depending on the Lord for my guidance, I believe that the story of Emmett Till will be perpetuated."

—Mamie Till Mobley
Mother of Emmett Till

"Well, I think that it so important to remember those who lost their lives in the struggle for equality and civil rights, many of whom also sacrificed their freedoms so that we would be able to live a better life. Unfortunately, we cannot go back in time to change history, but we can examine the social infrastructures that helped to create a climate of social hate that served to undermine the future of Black Americans yet time and time again. By providing our youth with many different viewpoints, stories and experiences from the past; they will be better able to develop their own perceptions and vision of the future."

—E. Willa Simpson

FINAL THOUGHTS AND DEDICATION PAGES

By . . . E. Willa Simpson

REMEMBERING MY BROTHER

The night before my youngest brother's death, I was touched with the vision of a funeral. However, I never imagined that it would be his. Unwilling to accept the reality that God had placed before me, I thought that I was just being overly concerned about my Grandparents growing older. I had no idea that the death that I had sensed would in fact be that of my youngest brother, to occur only a few short hours later. I also had no idea that my brother had traveled out of town to the Grand Canyon for the weekend with some friends and I could never possibly imagine how the days to follow that one terribly frightening night would change the rest of my life forever.

In my own personal experience, I do believe very strongly in the existence of a higher being . . . God. It is truly amazing to witness how gentle His love can be in an experience as emotionally devastating as the loss of a loved one. It is truly remarkable that at a time when it feels like we are being punished, that God is in essence, actually there all of the time. I myself only came to this realization through the wisdom and inner knowledge that I achieved after many long conversations with my father that were related to my brother's death.

Three days prior to my brother's passing, I started singing this song subconsciously over and over again. Most are familiar with this song as being the theme to the highly acclaimed motion picture, "The Color Purple." Its intriguing lyrics proclaim, "Maybe God is trying to tell me something." While speaking to a friend over the telephone, I distinctly recall singing this song. When we both recognized it to be a gospel song, we became unusually amused at the thought, especially when considering that I had not been inside the doors of a church for quite some time. And little did I know what God had in store for me, my family or my life.

On Tuesday morning I went back to work and tried as hard as possible to forget about the divine revelation from the previous night. But not for long . . . the phone rang. Unlike my normal routine, I did not pick it up. I just sat there . . . staring. A co-worker noticed my hesitation and quickly picked up the telephone. She informed me that it was my parents. I felt completely immobilized as the vision of the previous night began to re-surface. I began to think to myself silently, "No, not Big Mama or Big Daddy. Please God, not now!" I hesitated a few brief moments longer and slowly picked up the telephone. It was Daddy. He told me that he would be there immediately, and even though I'm sure that it probably took him no long than his usual fifteen minutes, it seemed like an eternity and I guess it was . . . my little brother's.

Daddy walked hesitantly into my office, held me in his arms tightly and told me for the first time that my brother Rex had gone away for the weekend with some friends, he had been in an accident and he was in critical condition. It seemed almost like how I would imagine an out of body experience to be. I felt light. I just didn't feel there. His words were echoing and time slowed down. Next thing I knew, I was standing outside of the building and he was holding me up. I felt like I couldn't breathe. To this day, I still don't remember that long walk outside.

We immediately located the rest of the family and drove to the Palm Springs hospital where my brother had been taken. It was quite a drive from Long Beach, California. I apologize for not being anymore specific. But for me, time would never be the same.

We parked in a fire lane when we finally reached the hospital and I burst through the emergency room doors. I was the first one. I began to ask the receptionist where my brother would be, but it just wouldn't come out. I was trembling. Daddy took over immediately and we were directed to what the hospital referred to as the "Quiet Room." I should have known then. He was gone. The surgeon came in and confirmed it. He even massaged my brother's heart. He said that he thought he could save him.

My family cried out, the heavens opened up and my reply was an angry "No!" as I burst out of the room, the front doors of the hospital and down the road. Running until my legs gave out, but someone caught me. It was John, my older brother.

Losing my youngest brother and laying him down to rest was indeed the hardest experience that I have gone through in my entire life. It seems that so often as African American people, we do not prepare for these types of unexpected and inevitable events. Therefore, it is more common that we perceive death as something negative . . . an ending. We must begin to deal more successfully and positively concerning the passing away of a loved one.

My brother was only twenty years old! He was bright and eager to claim his rightful inheritance to this nation as a Black man and determined to love men and women of all ethnic diversities. He was a beautiful person both inside and out, dedicated to all people, humble in spirit and compassionate; quite similar to the personality of our mother.

I have never in all of my life been more aware of the bright existence of angels that walk the Earth remarkably unrecognized. I like so many others was terribly unprepared for the loss of my brother's life; however he has truly touched my life with many precious gifts since the time of his passing away.

Rex believed in life, the quality of living and loving as a people. Only moments before his death, he remarked to his friends while watching the sunrise on the side of a lonely desert road, of how it reminded him that we ought to appreciate the small things in life. The wisdom of this statement finalized the last moments of my brother's life as we knew it. But through the deep love of God, his passing was not merely a new entry into my heavenly Father's book of life, but also a deeper personal expression for myself. It completed the circle of my brother's life.

Rex loved people to a degree that he left us all with the knowledge, wisdom and love to be able to pick up and carry on. He touched our lives with the inspiration to achieve our own dreams until our paths meet again.

It seems that since the beginning of time, God's children strived to be in tune with the spiritual. They talked to God and they believed that he answered. The Lord sent them angels in dreams and they received them. And for myself, a little brother to love and so . . . I loved him.

When you lose someone, make sure that you leave your heart, spirit, mind and soul open to receive them, along with the deep love of God so that you can acquire a deeper understanding of self. *For we must learn to let go of those things that we can no longer hold, and carry with us always the knowledge of those things that we hold to be most precious. For the love of God manifested is like an ever-present rainbow.* If you do these things faithfully then you will see, that out of the darkness comes such a great light, that it reminds us constantly that we do not lose our loved ones forever. God Bless!

AND WHEN I THINK
OF SUNRISES . . .

Only moments before my youngest brother's accident, he explained to his friends while watching the sunrise on the side of a lonely desert road, of how it reminded him that we ought to appreciate the small things in life. I can only hope that this poem will do my brother's last thoughts justice. Because just like the color of purple, even the sunrises want to be loved.

And when I think of sunrises, little brother
I will always think of you.

The things that most live to take for granted,
You realized could all end soon.

And I don't want to say goodbye, little brother
No, I don't want to leave you.

But traveling deep down inside my soul,
I just don't know what else to do.

For the road is long and greatly traveled,
That this family must now go.

But little brother, my strong Black brother
In our hearts remains your soul.

Footsteps walking through time, into eternity.
But Lord, oh Lord, we just couldn't see.

That God had something better
Waiting there in heaven for you.

I feel that we've been left behind.
And yet, silently
In a prayer
I wait to see you again soon.

If I could shake the shackles of time
And open up the doors of heaven
To take you back into the only life I've ever known with you
I would do this for you, little brother.

But for now
My eyes do cry.
And I ask myself why it is indeed,
That we must say goodbye.

But even still
I know that it must be so.
And if I couldn't help you,
Nor bring you peace,
On the side of that lonely, desolate desert road
Then maybe I can now
By realizing and understanding that God is trying to tell me
something.

Because you heard him when he spoke
He opened up the doors of heaven
To carry you home.

But why, oh why
Do I feel so all alone.
Brother dearest,
Why?

We must learn to appreciate the ground beneath our feet,
The winds that caress our cheekbones,
The silence that prevails in a moment of triumph.
And the love that is shared between all beings, of nature and of human
existence.

And so, when I think of sunrises, little brother
I will always hold you near.
And I will not forget you,
I promise.

From now and forever you are to be found within every tear that I cry,
And you little brother alone will be the sunrise that never sets and
never dies.

For you see, my brother believed in inner pride and dignity;
As individuals, as a race, as well as races interacting amongst one
another.

We must come together and cease from fulfilling the stereotypes that
others have set for us.

I love you brother.

FOR MAMA

You gave me life
And raised me up,
Taught me the way to go.

Gave me someone
That I could love,
A never ending road.

You held my hands
When times were rough,
Wiped all the tears I cried.

You listened close
When problems came
And gave the best advice.

You gave me love
Without an end
Although I made mistakes.

You picked me up
Patched up my wounds
And somehow felt my pain.

You watched the men
I loved so much.
You saw them come and go.

When I was weak
You gave me strength
When I just could not let go.

When I was sick
You doctored and nursed me
You waited patiently by my side.

When brother passed
You understood my sorrow.
You knew how I felt inside.

I have loved you
And I have needed you.
You were never too far away
From me.

I am thankful for you mama.
I am thankful for the time we've shared
And especially the memories.

You gave me a love of which
I could depend
And the faith to see me through

The disappointments
That this life would bring
And distance when I needed room.

You loved me enough
To tell me the truth
When you knew that I would turn away.

Crowned resentment with patience,
Bitterness with love
And when all else failed . . .
You prayed.

When I think of mansions
I think of mama
And all that she has prepared for me.

E. Willa Simpson

I could never hope to understand tomorrow
In the same way that my mother knows
Her youngest daughter,
Like black wings that lift away
A lonesome eternity.

She moves me . . . .
I love you mom.

FOR DAD:

When I think about what it means,
about what it takes
to be a real man . . .
I will always have the example
of my father.

I didn't have a deadbeat dad
an absentee father
or a chump.

I had a father
in the true sense of the word;
a real man
who not only created
but also raised me,
not only nurtured,
but he also praised me.

He was there for all of the ups
and downs.
He was around
for all of the disappointments
and tragedies
that this life has to offer,
and I know this
because I am his daughter.

He accepted all of the joys
and pains
of being a dad . . .
The appreciation,
and the lack of,
the good times,

along with the bad,
both happy times,
and sad.
He accepted all of the consequences
of being a dad.

He didn't walk out on us when times got rough.
He accepted the harsh words
that sometimes flew out
in anger.
The setbacks and the disappointments
of being a dad.
and you know what . . .
he forgave me.
He sacrificed and often felt
that no one noticed . . .
or even cared.

And still . . .
he was there.

When I think about what it means
and what it takes to be a real man
I get down on my knees
and give thanks to the Living God
because I will always have the example
of my Dad.

FOR STEVIE WONDER . . .

The most beautiful words
i ever heard
were spoken out of the lips
of a Black man.

*Dedicated to the beloved Stevie Wonder who fought tirelessly to
ensure that Dr. Martin Luther King Jr.'s birthday would be observed as
a National holiday . . . *We will not forget you!*

And a special thank you to my beloved *"Big Mama"* who trusted me with the only picture she had of her mother, my Great Grandmother (Cover Photo). Thank you for all of the sacrifices that you and Big Daddy endured to make us the family that we are today. *I will always love you!*

MANY SPECIAL THANKS TO:

Mamie Till Mobley
Angela Davis
Michael Eric Dyson
Howard Bingham
Ernest Whithers
And to God
. . . for making this work possible.

To Daddy and Rex, with love . . . until.

REX SIMPSON REMEMBERED ...

Rex Simpson, my brother and best friend died in his senior year of studies at UCLA attending under partial scholarship from the late "Johnnie Cochran," majoring in political science and with dreams of completing his graduate studies with a civil rights law degree from UCLA. His life was cut short on August 3, 1993 due to a tragic car accident, but his dream is still realized through the **Rex Simpson Memorial Scholarship Fund** which benefits African American students who also have dreams of one day attending UCLA. For more information, please contact the UCLA Foundation at (310)794-3193. *He will forever be greatly missed.*

ABOUT THE AUTHOR

E. Willa Simpson is a longtime advocate for civil rights and justice; formerly residing on the local advisory committee of the *"Tavis Smiley"* Foundation. Simpson's many accomplishments include film and television production, in addition to several photo journalism credits, receiving national acclaim. Simpson recently released a documentary film entitled "The Lynching Tree" featuring political activist Angela Davis and is currently working on several other upcoming literary and theatrical projects.

www.ingramcontent.com/pod-product-compliance
Lightning Source LLC
Chambersburg PA
CBHW051445280526
45785CB00003B/1434